We Will Dance Again

We Will Dance Again

A Mother's Love Letter to Her Son

Dianne Sauter

Copyright © 2016 by Dianne Sauter.

Library of Congress Control Number:		2016902036
ISBN:	Hardcover	978-1-5144-5825-9
	Softcover	978-1-5144-5824-2
	eBook	978-1-5144-5823-5

All rights reserved. No part of this book may be reproduced or transmitted in any form or by any means, electronic or mechanical, including photocopying, recording, or by any information storage and retrieval system, without permission in writing from the copyright owner.

Any people depicted in stock imagery provided by Thinkstock are models, and such images are being used for illustrative purposes only. Certain stock imagery © Thinkstock.

Print information available on the last page.

Rev. date: 02/18/2016

To order additional copies of this book, contact:
Xlibris
1-888-795-4274
www.Xlibris.com
Orders@Xlibris.com
734592

PREFACE

Ever since I decided to write this book, I thought it would encourage others, but at the same time, negative thoughts have sometimes kept me from believing it would happen. But this motivated me even more. God will get the glory!

Journal

This is the true account of my journey with my son, Michael, 23 years of age, a journey that would shake my life to the core. Most of this was documented in a journal for him to read, for when he recovered. I share this, hoping that this experience will be a strength and encouragement to others who have gone through a similar experience, and even for those who have not, to be reminded of how precious our lives are to each other, and how God is in the midst of it all.

Dear Michael, I have recorded your journey through this tragic accident, in the hopes that when you awake, you would be encouraged by your progress. I have written it from my heart and my own understanding of the circumstances. Some of the events may be sporadic or not in order, as I was in a state of shock, still trying to process what was happening to you. "God have mercy!"

ACKNOWLEDGEMENTS

Thank you for your support:

To Diane Kirkwood, my best friend, who journeyed daily with me during Michael's time in the hospital and the months that followed. Her dedication to seeing me through was a strength that was possible only through God.

To my new friend, Rochelle Sato, who without her help, support and relentless commitment, this book would not have been possible.

To my older sons, Shane and Daniel. I am thankful for the strength they gave, the encouragement, support and love they gave to me, even through their own pain of seeing their little brother suffering. They held me in their arms, showing more concern about me than themselves. They are amazing boys. I am so proud of them.

Thank you to my daughter-in-law, Sari, for the beautiful scrapbook about Michael. Also, she and her mother made my coming home so much easier, with framed and enlarged photos of Michael and me, along with extra things to brighten up my apartment after his death.

To all of Michael's friends and family who prayed and stood by his side....their names are too numerous to mention, but remain in my heart....thank you.

Other family members and other friends were supportive and helpful. I felt very thankful that they were "there" for Michael. Most of their names are not mentioned, nor were their journal entries published, in order to protect their anonymity.

FOREWORD

The verses and passages that are written in this book are ones meant to comfort Michael and perhaps help with my own sanity. I believe that my son, Michael, was aware of what was happening to him. And I believe he was relieved to know that he was finally going home to heaven. The words I spoke, the prayers I prayed, and the love I gave strengthened him for that wonderful day.

Michael was a passenger in a vehicle with a co-worker/friend in a truck, on their way to work. The driver fell asleep and the truck rolled onto its side. After the accident, Michael was conscious and trying to get out of the truck, but could not move his legs. He asked his friend to help him out. Since he was not hurt badly, his friend was able to help him out of the truck. From there, he was airlifted to Vancouver General Hospital.

September 22

The news

It was Sunday, September 22, 2013, approximately 10 a.m. when I received a text from my oldest son, Shane, asking me if he could stop in for a minute. I told him to just come in, the door would be unlocked. I was sitting at my kitchen table when he walked in, as if in a hurry, and sat down on the couch. He asked me to come sit for a minute. My heart immediately started to beat fast. I knew something bad had happened. As I sat beside him, searching his face for an answer, I could see the confused look of horror on his face as he struggled to speak. I said loudly, "What? What?" As he tried to get the words out, "It's Michael!"

I said, "What about Michael? Is he okay, is he alive?" He nodded yes, "Michael has been in an accident. He can't move his legs." My hands started to shake. I was trying hard to process this nightmare. I started to pace, thinking I needed to get to him.

I was able to speak to Michael on the phone as he was being airlifted to Vancouver General Hospital. I was so glad to hear his voice. I told him that I loved him and that I was driving immediately to see him and would be there in a few hours. He told me that he loved me too, and to drive safe. I was so thankful that I could speak to my precious son. My only concern now was to get to him as soon as possible.

The drive

It was before noon and I needed to drive straight through into the night. The drive would take me approximately 12 hours. It would be 2 a.m. when I would arrive. I don't drive at night very much, because my sight isn't the best. And today it was raining too. But I knew God was with me. I had no fear. I rehearsed Joshua 1:9, "Have I not commanded you to be strong and courageous? Do not tremble or be dismayed. The Lord your God is with you wherever you go" (ASB).

God was my comfort, and my eyes. I had two CDs of Charles Stanley and I played them over and over, for 12 hours. He is a preacher that I listen to online. The CDs were titled, "Dressed for the battle." I knew this was going to be a battle to get through too. The CDs helped me stay focused on the Lord.

I didn't know how serious the accident was. There was a lot going through my mind, but I trusted God and focused on God's power to keep me strong. God kept me calm.

I knew that Michael was a passenger in the vehicle, and that he wasn't responsible for the accident, but I forgave the driver. I prayed that God would be his strength. I wanted to be able to meet with him someday to tell him that I forgive him and that God loves him.

I wasn't assuming anything about the accident, even though I could have thought the worst. Maybe Michael's legs were just temporarily hurt, and he might need rehabilitation. But those thoughts made me anxious. I quickly asked God to hold me tight in his loving arms, as I continued to trust him. There were two things I was sure about, that God would see us (Michael and I) through this, and secondly, that we would help others that were possibly going through similar circumstances.

"This wasn't supposed to happen, Michael." Remember, we were looking forward to seeing each other in October at the Calgary Airport. We were counting down the days. We were so excited. Shane and your precious nephew, Aedan, and I would be there, waiting for you.

September 23

The arrival

When I arrived, it was 2 a.m. and it was dark and raining. I had never been to Vancouver General Hospital, and I didn't know where to go, so I pulled up to the Emergency Department. The receptionist was very kind. When I told her my son was there, she came right outside and showed me where I could park. I did so, and she came with me to the floor Michael would be on. I went to the waiting room of the ICU, where I waited for news of my son. I am not sure how long I waited. It seemed many, many hours.

5 AM - The prognosis from the surgeon

The surgeon came to the ICU waiting room. I was still trying to process where I was. As he was speaking, it felt like he was speaking in slow motion. He said that Michael's spinal cord was damaged, and he was in surgery for eight hours. He said that he saw Michael's injury as very serious. He came right out and said that Michael's injury did not look good. The vertebrae he could mend, but the spinal cord itself was seriously damaged. I thought I could not be hearing what I thought I was hearing, so I asked the doctor to repeat it.

"Oh my God, my baby was in trouble and I ached to see him."

The doctor said I could see Michael in a while. That was the last thing I remember, until I finally leaned over my baby and told him I loved him, and I would be here while he was recuperating. He nodded. As I left his side, I fell apart.

"God please… I know you are with Michael and with whatever strength he has left, help Michael to trust in you in this very serious situation."

I noticed that he had stitches on his forehead from the impact of the accident. I thought to myself that even if Michael couldn't walk, was in a wheelchair and needed rehab, he would come out of this after all. He was physically strong, determined and more committed than anyone I knew. But of course, I wanted him well enough to walk again.

September 24

Today, you are making progress. You are basically breathing on your own, with minimal oxygen from a respirator.

The doctor showed me the x-ray results before and after your surgery, and your vertebrae are all lined up after an eight-hour procedure on the front and back of your neck. There were four screws to hold them in place, so there were two incisions. You are strong, fit, and with no infections or side-effects. The doctor said you are doing well. Tomorrow will be even more progress. God is with you.

September 25

The complications

This is the day when I realized that things were not going to be so simple. When I walked in to see you this morning, you were packed in ice. The nurse said your temperature went way up, which they said was critical, but the doctors were working hard to bring it back down again. They sedated you. Your body has swelled up, especially from your waist down.

"My little Star, where are you?"

I prayed over you this morning. I prayed that God would bring your temperature down. You are in God's hands, even though things seem to be out of control.

"Dear God please heal my son."

Later in the day, your temperature came down a bit, and then it went back up again. From what I understand, the doctor thought maybe you were allergic to the anesthetic and/or experiencing "malignant hypothermia." They were not sure what caused your temperature to go up. The doctors wanted to flush your body and replace it with new medications that would stabilize you.

Again, we need to get over this hurdle, another 24- hour period of waiting for your continued recovery. I need to see you, to speak to you, knowing you can hear me. I only see you sedated and cold. I only see you suffering. I can't take seeing you this way.

When I am with you, I cry silently, turning away, telling you I have to blow my nose, and that I have a cold, so that you don't worry. I encourage you, even if I don't think you can hear me, or can you? I am confused about that.

The breathing tube was so uncomfortable that you tried to pull it out. The nurses said that they told you to stop trying to take the tube out, that they said you would die, so you stopped, but only for that moment.

"It must have been so uncomfortable, Sweetie. The nurses had to tie your wrists to the bed. This is how we knew you had movements in your upper body, but you were unable to move your fingers."

"Oh Lord, please help Michael. Take his fear away, so that he can trust in you. Help me to be strong for my son."

My sweet little Micheal - I LOVE you!
Am praying for a miracle for you, I think we are going to get it.
All your aunts & uncles said to say hi and tell you they are praying for you. I will be back to see you in a few days. This is your cool aunt signing off for now. Love you.
Auntie Elsie ♡

Sept 25 2013
Wednesday

Michael (Super Carrier)
Only a temporary set back for a boy who knows nothing except love and honesty, especially to his Lord and family. We will be patient for you to heal, as we know you will. We love you so much, I am so lucky to have a nephew like you. I can hardly wait to talk to you again, soon! Stay strong as you are the strongest of all!!

Love Uncle D.

Hey Brother, you're an amazing person and a inspiration to so many people. You're going to do so many great things in your life, I can't wait to see that. I'm always here for you and, I know I don't say it but I love you very much. Keep kicking ass and show these guys here what you can do. You have made me look at things differently and shown me not to take anything for granted.

I am so proud of you you have no idea how much. Stay positive if I would have to choose anyone in this world that could get through this I would choose you. You're the man! Love your brother Shane

Dear Munch; This is your dearest auntie Annette + Uncle Mike came to see you!! We know you are going to come around from this terrible terrible tragic memory in your life, you will be able to smile again and laugh. Please hurry-up and get better so you can do great things with your life and help others see there is a purpose for you living this accident.

Your little cousins Addison and Brooklyn are so worried about you, we pray every night before bed so God blesses you extra special. Addison asks me everyday how are you and "is his "BIG COUSIN" better be OK. Brook asked too. "Cousin Better," she says, hoping I will say "YES". So U Better B" OK Michael, your little cousins love you and are praying every da

Hey Michael, your uncle Kevin is here waiting for you to heal up & say hi! You are one strong young man that has touched many hearts including mine! We all love you sooo much & pray to God that you get healthy real soon. Melissa & Jermaine send their prayers and hope to see you well real soon. I can't wait until you can give Kiana a ride on your huge shoulders again.

We are all here for you. Love you a ton Michael.

Michael and Nephew Aedan

September 26

Daniel had started a new job in Edmonton, but he has decided to stay here with you. He reads the Bible to you daily and goes in every evening just before midnight, to check on you and say good-night, after visiting hours are over.

Michael, you have no idea how many lives you are changing because of this very difficult time in such a short time. You have brought families together and mended hearts and relationships. Daniel has become more forgiving of himself and others. Uncle Kevin, said that he was "a changed man," as we cried together in the hospital. At the time, he put himself in my shoes. He saw that he had been putting himself before others, now realizing the importance of family, especially his daughter, Kiana. She still has a picture on her wall, of you holding her on your shoulders. We all thought that if anyone could make it through this struggle, you would, because of your physical fitness, positive attitude and your faith. And regardless of your outcome, Kevin now has more empathy and faith.

I know that other people's lives are also changed, especially from reading their comments in my journal. Our favourite nurse, Ellen, was wonderful with your care. As she went about her work, she spoke to you as if you could hear, and called you "honey."

This morning you seem to be doing better, your blood pressure and temperature has stabilized, although you are still heavily sedated.

I want so much to talk to you, Michael, and for you to talk to me. I have been telling you how you are jumping over hurdles in your recovery, to encourage you. And I believe that you hear me.

I read Bible verses to you every day to strengthen you. Joshua 1:9 is one of our favorites.

"Dear God, help Michael through this."

I am with you Michael, every day, many times during the day and evening, before you sleep. Before I go to bed, I pray and cry. But God is good. He is with us always. It is his power within us that sustains us each day.

The nurse said you had hiccups last night. I somehow found strength in that. For so long, I have wanted to see some normalcy--for lack of a better word--in your recovery.

I was telling the nurses that once you get the breathing tube out and are able to talk, that they will just love your personality, your love, your humorous side, and that they will always remember when they cared for you and helped see you through this journey on to an amazing life ahead.

Throughout this day, I have been in to see you many times, as the nurses keep sending me out of your room so they can care for you, when they bathe you, or turn you over, or take more tests. Every day the doctors and students studying medicine make the rounds, usually between 7:30 and 8:30 a.m., and again at 7 to 8:30 p.m. I have to use the intercom if I want to see you, and a lot of times, the nurses will say that I should come back in half an hour. So I will go back again, waiting to see you every hour, every minute. I never wanted to leave your side... looking for little hints of you.

I would just stand over you and caress your chest, as if to give you a hug. I put my hand on your forehead to close your eyes. You loved that so much when you were very young.

"My precious little Star."

The doctor said this evening that you are progressing. I am not sure what that really means. They explain it, but I sometimes can't process it, but I do hear the "progress" part.

It's still too unbelievable that this is really happening to you. It's 6 p.m., and I am still waiting to see your beautiful blue eyes. The doctor said you were slowly progressing, but you were not "out of the woods" yet. There was a big meeting with the respiratory therapist, the surgeon, nurses and rehabilitation doctor. Because of all the complications in your recovery, the go-ahead for rehabilitation is, of course, unattainable at this time. We need to get you well first. And it will be a difficult challenge.

I read to you today, "He who dwells in the shelter of the Most High will abide in the shadow of the Almighty. I will say to the Lord, 'My refuge and my fortress, my God, in whom I trust!'" (Psalm 91:1-2, ASB).

Great news! The doctors took you off two of the three medications you were on, so your eyes will be open in the morning!

"Thank you, God."

"I am calling everyone about the good news about you, Sweetie! Tomorrow morning we expect your eyes to be open and engaging."

"Thank you Jesus!"

I am getting ready to see you this morning. My hotel room that I am staying in, is only two short blocks from the hospital, so I pick up my coffee at Tim Horton's, which is right on the way. It's 8:30. When I got to the intercom to ask to be let in to see you, the nurse said to come back. Now, I am worried that something has gone wrong. Finally, I am let in. I noticed right away that your eyes were *not open*. The doctor told me you had another setback and you had to be sedated again....internal complications, kidney function, heart rate, blood pressure are constantly monitored.

"My God, my God, what is going on?"

It has been five days! I feel I can't handle these setbacks, not to mention the frustration and pain that you, Michael, have to endure. I pray that you are not in pain.

"God have mercy! You are the Great Physician."

"Michael, I cried to God that you will get through this."

"Please Lord, bring Michael back."

While I was with you, the doctors took you off sedation meds again. Your eyes slowly started to open. They will give you less oxygen and see if you can breathe a bit more on your own. I see these "speed bumps" along the way, Sweetie, and I see you are fighting the best you can.

"I am so proud of you. God is with you."

I am usually at the hospital at 8:30 a.m., just after the doctors' early rounds and their shift change, so new staff have an update of what has gone on with you in the night. Sometimes they will send me out for half an hour, so they can turn you, which they do a couple of times during the day and night. I usually stand behind the curtain or leave the room. It takes four nurses to lift you, two on each side, because you are such a big boy. When I finally got to see you, your eyes were open just slightly but did not focus. It is so hard to know if you know that I'm here. But I talk to you and encourage you, read the Bible, and pray with you, like you can hear me. I pray you can.

From what I understand, the doctor said that the hypothermia that you encountered, if indeed that's what it is, is extremely rare. So what you are doing is teaching the doctors how to remedy this condition. But the doctors don't know how to treat it fast enough to help you. *It seems your health has gone down since day one.*

"Oh my God. Show the doctors what to do. I pray my son is getting better. My heart aches for him."

The respiratory therapist comes in every couple of days to try and loosen up your chest so you are able to cough up, from the build-up in your lungs. I can't watch because the nurse presses hard on your stomach and shakes your chest. It's too difficult to hear and see you so vulnerable and helpless.

September 28

This morning, when I came in to see you, the nurse said your heart rate wasn't what it should be during the night. I asked to see the cardiologist and he said that your heart was damaged due to your body trauma. You had to be totally sedated again throughout the night. This is so scary, my precious son. I am so worried but still trusting God.

I say to you,

"Please, please, please Michael, get better."

"Oh my Lord, what is happening? Is my son in pain? The gut-wrenching thoughts are unbearable. Jesus help. Please find him for me, Lord."

The doctor has put you on heart medication. He also said there is muscle breakdown in your body, and they don't know why. I read to you today, "Hear my cry, O God, attend unto my prayer. From the end of the earth I will cry unto thee, when my heart is overwhelmed lead me to the rock that is higher than I" (Psalm 61:1-2, KJV).

"Praise you Jesus, in this storm."

The doctor has taken you off the sedation meds, so that eventually, you can breathe on your own and take that breathing tube out. I need to see that you see me, hear me, and talk to me.

"Where are you, my son? I need you desperately to get better. God is working, I know."

September 29

The nurse is trying to put a new line into your vein, which is hard to watch, because your entire body is swollen up, so that you cannot see any veins anywhere. They need to have a quicker way to administer meds, by doing this.

Later in the day, I could see you only a short time. The doctors are sedating you a bit because of your blood pressure again. But your eyes are open and you are trying to move your arms. Very hopeful... but can you see me?? Your eyes seem to be searching for my voice.

"Oh God, help Michael. Help me help him. What can I do?"

"I know you hear me, Michael. I am here. God has lifted you up with his righteous right hand."

In the evening, your beautiful blue eyes are open... but you cannot see or focus... *"Why, why? What is going on?"*

The doctors say that it will take some time and that you need to be stable in all areas of your body. Being sedated so much had to be done, until all your vitals are stable. I still don't understand. The doctors took a CAT scan and an ultrasound, and they said they were normal, so what's this all about? I am frustrated.

"I love you, Sweetie, so much. This is a living nightmare. I would sleep in your room if they would let me, just so I could be with you in the night, to comfort you when you couldn't sleep."

This evening, the nurses have a water mattress on you, because your temperature went way up again. Your kidneys are not functioning like they should be, so the doctors are trying to figure out why. There are so many unanswered questions, and if the doctors can't figure it out, then who can? God can. I suggested to the doctors to find doctors from different countries to be contacted. The only one they contacted so far was from Toronto. No answers from them, either.

"I am so frustrated... Lord, please help!"

The doctors say you are progressing slowly, but where is this progress? "Still not out of the woods," they said. It seems like you are getting worse every day. God is with you. In the evening, the doctor spoke about your muscles and the breakdown that was happening. The doctors are still searching to understand why this is happening. Another CT scan will be taken. They hope they don't find anything, and if not, they want to take an MRI. The doctors say that they are trying to do everything possible, to find out why these problems are happening. There have been many meetings with the doctors. I believe they are doing all they know to do.

"God have mercy."

Your case, Michael, has never been seen by many of the doctors here in the VGH. That's what the doctors say. So your case definitely is helping them find new solutions in medicine. God is using you in extraordinary ways. Not only medically, but through personal lives.

"Your family and friends are coming together because of you, Sweetie. Keep fighting; the Lord is with you, my Star."

7 PM

You went to have a CAT scan. I waited for you to pass by in the hallway before you went in, my precious Michael.

"God is with you."

September 30

Today is a new day. You are getting better….and God is good.

"He has you, Michael; He is the Great Healer, the Great Physician. Praise Him!"

This morning the nurses weaned you off the sedatives and you were wide-awake. By that, I mean your eyes were open and you were trying to move your arms. But your wrists were tied. Your eyes were searching for me. I know you could hear me, but you still could not speak or see me.

"God, please make Michael see. This really worries me, Lord, why can't Michael see me?"

As I kissed you and cradled your face to mine, I quoted Psalm 23, "The Lord is my shepherd…" and, "Have I not commanded you, be strong and courageous, do not tremble or be dismayed for the Lord your God is with you wherever you go" (Joshua 1:9). I prayed with you as I do every day.

"God, have mercy."

2:30 PM

This afternoon you look so uncomfortable. The breathing tube looked like you were gagging on it. Oh, my God, to see your agony! My baby, helpless.

I asked the nurse to give you something for pain because you looked very uncomfortable. I see progress in some ways, but in other ways, I don't see progress, and I am expecting a miracle. Soon, I pray, the doctors will say you are doing great!

6:45 PM

The doctors are going to place a "trach." This is a breathing tube that is surgically placed directly into your throat. So now you won't be gagging on a breathing tube in your mouth.

"God, have mercy."

I read to you today, "And whatsoever ye shall ask in my name, that will I do that the Father may be glorified in the Son. If ye shall ask anything in my name I will do it" (John 14:13-14, KJV).

See you in the morning, my Star.

October 1

"I love you so much, Michael."

"Thank you, God for healing Michael. I claimed it before and I continue to claim it. Be it your will, Lord, for you will be glorified, Lord."

This morning that cool air mattress was on your body from your neck down. I know you are already cool. (I know you would laugh at that comment if you could.) I read to you Matthew 17:20, "If you have faith as a mustard seed, you shall say to the mountain, move from here to there, and it shall move and nothing shall be impossible to you."

I spoke to the doctor and your spine specialist, and your nurse. They all gave updates on your progress. They are mainly concerned with your temperature and why your muscles are breaking down. Today you look better than yesterday and what I mean by that is, your face is clear, your eyes are open, and you are awake. But you still cannot see me. This is what is so difficult.

I know you know that I'm here with you and I am talking to you. Telling you what is going on with your progress. It is slow, but it's still progress. Your MRI is tomorrow. We will know more.

"God have mercy!"

October 2

I'm leaning in toward you every day to speak God's love for you and how he is with you, and repeating Joshua 1:9. I got pictures of you and Aedan enlarged at a drugstore and hung them on your ICU room window. I know how much you love Shane's little guy, Aedan. He looks so tiny beside you where you are holding him in your arms! We had a great visit today. I read God's word to you and we prayed. Many cards from others have been placed on your window sill. Some of your family and friends have written words of love and encouragement to you. Enclosed, are just a few of them. The nurses just love them.

My hand is in yours every day. As I entwine my fingers in yours, I am reminded of how you always took my hand in yours, to warm them up.

"Oh Lord, help me through this."

Your temperature went up again, but it came down as the cool mattress was placed over you again. You were moving your arm a bit this morning. So that is a good day. The nurse called your name and asked you to open your eyes and you did. You weren't able to focus yet, but it's coming. I know that you are totally aware that I am here. Sometimes, I doubt that you can hear me, but am soon reminded that you can. I am looking for any little glimmer of hope that you are here with me, as I show my love and encouragement for you. You have been sedated so many times because of all your unstable vital signs.

I am staying with you, Michael, until the end, whatever that might be. I am here to help you through your rehabilitation. I am giving notice to my landlady back in Airdrie, that I am going to move to Vancouver as soon as possible.

Today, all of your visitors had to wear gowns and gloves, because there were some bacteria in the ICU.

It's hard to tell if you are trying to talk, or if you are saying you are hurting, so I always tell the nurse so that she can try to make you comfortable. To see you in pain and discomfort is unbearable every day, and it is every minute of every day. When I am away from you, you are all I think about.

"God give me strength to be strong for Michael."

You try to move your arms, even though your wrists are tied down.

"God have mercy."

I hug you, with my head on your chest, and arms on your shoulders, and I tell you that I am hugging you and I tell you that you are telling me not to worry and that you love me....I know you would want me to know that. I love you "tons and tons."

"God have mercy."

"I tell you that I can't even imagine, Sweetie, how you must feel, not being able to express yourself."

You are getting an MRI at 2 p.m., so I will see you after rounds tonight. More tests were taken earlier today and your kidney function is still a problem. So the doctor said that possibly short-term dialysis, to flush out toxins, should help. Later on in the day, things are stabilizing in that area. Great news!

All of these wires, instruments, monitors and machines, gauging your body functions, your temperature, blood pressure, heart rate, kidney function, your breathing, medicine intake, and probably a lot more than what I see, are all keeping you going.

"God have mercy!"

8:30 PM

I read to you today: "Oh, love the Lord, all ye His saints for the Lord preserveth the faithful and plentifully rewardeth the proud doer. Be of good courage and He shall strengthen your heart, all ye that hope in the Lord....Oh love the Lord, all ye his saints, for the LORD preserveth the faithful, and plentifully rewardeth the proud doer. Be of good courage, and he shall strengthen your heart, all ye that hope in the LORD" (Psalm 31:23-24, KJV).

It's evening now, no MRI results yet. I am thinking, if there was a problem, we would have heard by now. No news is good news. Michael, we all see progress and promise.

Your brothers and I are sharing a room at a hotel just two blocks from VGH. It's so handy to be so close to you.

I break down every day, every night. At my hotel room, I call everyone and let them know of your complications and progress. There are so many friends and relatives that love you and are praying for you.

October 3

This morning when I came in, the nurse said that you had a rough night, that you hadn't had a lot of rest. You were agitated and uncomfortable.

"Oh Lord my baby is suffering too much, please help! My aching heart is so overwhelmed with grief!"

I prayed with you, laying hands on you, encouraging you on how well you were doing in fighting this illness. Every morning, I walk into Tim Horton's, which is only two blocks from the hospital and two blocks from my hotel.

But this particular morning, I sat down by the window, watching people walk to work and seeing the traffic of the day. I began to question my thoughts about your health, Michael. It is so hard to see progress in one way in your healing, and in another area, a setback. I am confused. What is God doing? Testing my faith? I can't explain the fear I have in my gut that your outcome is not going to be good. This is the only time I have felt like this. And I became overwhelmed with grief. I needed to talk to God immediately.

I headed for the Tim Horton's bathroom, locked the door and fell to my knees and began crying uncontrollably. I said,

"Lord, I am afraid I will lose my son. As Abraham had obeyed You, Lord, to sacrifice his son Isaac, You said that Isaac would be saved, because then You knew Abraham was faithful in his sacrifice."

As I continued to tremble and weep, I told God,

"If it is Michael that you want, I give him to you, but as Isaac was saved, please save my son, Michael. I will continue to trust you, Lord. God have mercy!"

Awake in my hotel room this morning, there was a seagull I called "Gulligan," sitting on the ledge of our 16th floor suite. I dropped him a cookie. We (Daniel and I) took a video of him. Can't wait to show you, you will laugh like crazy when you see it.

I finally found a star-shaped ring (black and sparkly) that I wear to remind me of you, and your love and strength in this difficult journey. I love you so much!

Later in the afternoon, I spoke to the doctor about your MRI results. He said that it was clear! And your CK levels are evening out, so that's good. At least it's not getting worse. He did say there was some damage (muscle breakdown), but according to what I understand, it's now under control.

Sometimes, my emotions are at the edge of losing my mind. I have had to trust God, so that I won't go crazy. And he has been faithful. I read to you today, and reminded you of one of two of our favorite Bible verses, "Have I not commanded you, be strong and courageous. Do not tremble or be dismayed. The Lord your God is with you, wherever you go" (Joshua 1:9)....

"I pray that you are not afraid and that God is holding you peacefully in his arms, during this extremely hard time."

As soon as your Great Aunt Elsie and Uncle Rick found out about your accident, Michael, they offered me their home for me to live in, while you go through your rehabilitation at GF Strong Centre. It's right next door to VGH. I also gave notice to my landlady in Airdrie, AB, so that I could be near you. Everything pointed to your getting well. Shane and cousin, Rob, told me not to worry about my belongings, that they would pack, move or store my things, so my place in Airdrie can be rented out to someone else.

There are so many family and friends that have texted messages all day long, to see how you're doing. It is non-stop. Facebook is bombarded with get-well wishes and "prayer warriors" from all over the world. I can't wait to show you. God is healing you and I will continue to tell you that. I read the story about Jesus healing the blind man (Mark 8: 22-25), and, "And as for me, thou upholdest me in mine integrity, and settest me before thy face for ever. Blessed be the LORD God of Israel from everlasting, and to everlasting. Amen, and Amen" (Psalm 41:12-13, KJV).

The heart specialist said that your heart is stable. I pray it stays that way. I read Psalm 31 and Romans 8 to you this evening. The nurse is going to give you a sleeping pill tonight. He said your liver is healthy enough to do that. Also, your kidney function has stabilized. It's not quite where it should be yet. The doctors say we are not out of the woods yet.

Shane has been flying back and forth, from Airdrie to Vancouver, to see you, but decided to stay here with you….being at home, and just hearing about the updates on your progress was too stressful. I had taken a picture of you in the ICU and sent it to Shane before he came, but he couldn't look at it until the next day after he received it. He was so scared to see you hurt.

I know that you have been trying to talk to me, but that tube in your throat is in the way. Because of all the complications, you have to have it to breathe, because you can't breathe on your own yet. But you will.

"It's so hard to watch you struggle, Sweetie!" Every time I write, I am in tears, and I have to stop to wipe my tears, so I can see what I am writing.

"Lord, I pray that my Michael will be able to get the breathing tube out. God have mercy!"

October 5

I went to see you this morning. The nurses told me what had happened in the night.

"Oh my God! Michael, your heart stopped beating during the night and they had to do CPR on you."

"Oh God, I am so afraid. Help Michael."

"It's unbearable to see you suffering and I can't help you."

"Please God have mercy!"

3 PM

The neurologist was called by the doctor because your eye movements have been going side-to-side.

"Oh Lord, is my son even there now?"

The doctors seem to believe that you are there, but that your recovery will take time. But I have only seen setback, then okay, then improvement, then not okay.

"I am scared, Jesus."

The doctor has checked your awareness of presence. He ordered an EKG.

6 PM

The EKG came back fine. Your heart is stable. The nurse said that when you were moved to turn you, that your heart rate plummeted, but you were okay. *"What's going on? What do you mean, 'he's okay'? My son is slowly dying before my eyes."*

"God, I don't understand any of this!!!"

The verse I read to you, "As sorrowful, yet always rejoicing, as poor yet making many rich, as having nothing, yet possessing all things" (II Corinthians 6:10).

October 6

Sunday, 8:30 PM

After your surgery and into the ICU, your room number was 28. You shared it with two other patients. They moved you to a second room, bed number 23, that you also shared with two other patients. The last room was number 11, and it was a private room. I asked the nurse why you had to be moved so much. She said it was standard procedure, when new patients come in and out of ICU.

My beautiful son, your eyes were open this morning. I told you how much I loved you. I know you heard me but you just couldn't respond. You were struggling to move your mouth with that tube in your throat.

"It's so hard to see you like this, Michael."

"Lord, help my son."

The nurse said that you had a good night, meaning you slept. I asked you to follow my voice and I thought you did, but not really sure, because your eyes move back and forth.

"Oh, God..."

A new doctor came in today and he said things were moving along in the right direction and he said that if there are any more issues with your heart that they are better prepared.

"God, have mercy."

This evening, as I place my fingers between yours and hold them close to my face, I softly stroke your forehead as you gently close your eyes. I know you know I am here.

"Lord, thank you for helping us through. We are weak, Lord, we need your strength."

My precious Michael, what a trip we are on, a roller coaster of emotions. I love you so much, Sweetie. God is the Great Physician. I sang that song, "This little light of mine," to you. I didn't see a response, but I knew you heard me.

October 7

Today you are on full life support. The doctor said your CO_2 levels are up, so when those levels (by my understanding) come down, then you won't need so much help breathing.

The doctors decreased your heart medication by one-half and changed the medication too. It seems one step back, and two steps ahead, then one step back, and one ahead. It's crazy. But God is with us.

The doctor wants to do a biopsy on your muscles to see if he could find anything there that might be causing your muscle breakdown and your other problems, like your heart, temperature and kidneys. I know the doctors are doing the best they can, but when the doctors don't have answers to our questions, that's devastating. They should know, but in your particular case they don't. I continue to trust God, because he knows what he is doing.

"I pray to God..."

The issue of your temperature is still not under complete control. Your eyes this morning are completely open, but not engaged. I am sure you hear me.

"Oh, God, I pray that Michael can focus..."

"It's so hard to see you so helpless; my heart bleeds for you, my precious Michael."

"HELP, JESUS, HELP! My pain is so terribly unbearable."

October 8

Every morning, during my walk to the hospital, I spend the whole trip praying to God for you. I have many sleepless nights, but God is with us all.

"Heal Michael's heart, Lord, and every organ in his body."

So much was going on this morning. There are two other patients that share your room, so that could be why I couldn't see you until 11:30 am. So, as many times before, I paced the ICU floor. I go for coffee a lot, and sometimes I will go outside just to clear my head.

One night, Shane took me to a movie to give me a break. That was good to get out of the hospital, into the fresh air and to see the world again. Although throughout the movie, I couldn't escape the thoughts of you, Michael.

Some good news! The nurse told me that you were taken off your heart medication completely. As I was telling you of this good news…

"Oh, my God!"

Your heart rate plummeted and a "red alert" sounded and nurses from everywhere were scrambling to your side. I thought I was in a dream and began to shake, but was quickly escorted out by one of the nurses. Praying desperately, I reluctantly left your side. The nurse assured me that you would be OK. The nurse told me to come back in half an hour, but after 15 minutes, the nurse came to get me from the waiting room. I can't even explain what those 15 minutes were like. My heart cried out to God.

I caressed your face and told you that I loved you, and repeated one of our favorite verses. Joshua 1:9, "Have I not commanded you be strong and courageous, do not tremble or be dismayed, for the Lord your God is with you wherever you go.

"No words, Sweetheart....I can't express the gut- wrenching feeling I have."

I have never felt this, ever in my life. I feel like I am going to pass out, the stress is so intense.

"I want you back! Where are you?!!"

I read to you page 54 from your <u>Dear Jesus</u> book. One of the verses was Ephesians 6:16, "Take up the shield of faith with which you can extinguish all the flaming arrows of the evil one.

"Praise God...Have mercy, Lord..."

I read to you today, "Let the words of my mouth and the meditations of my heart be acceptable in thy sight, O LORD, my strength, and my redeemer" (Psalm 19:14, KJV).

Now the doctor is saying that you haven't been able to hear me talking to you and that your eye movements don't show that

45

you do. *"What?"* He says as far as hearing, there has not been any indication of any.

"God, please heal my son..."

I spoke to the doctor again this afternoon and he said that you were in a comatose state, even with your eyes open. I don't get that. But then he said it can be temporary. *"How temporary? This is craziness!"*

Doctors still don't know why your temperature keeps rising. They have started you on a different drug, to see if that helps.... I am still trusting God, even when it looks so bad. He can, He will, change all that! I disagree with the doctors and believe that you can hear me and feel me with you.

"God, You promised, to use me and my children for your glory!"

The night before the accident, I was sitting in my rocker at home, feeling so content and happy with my life. I had a job I loved, a home that I loved, and good relationships with my family. I thanked the Lord and asked him what would be next in my life. I'd never done this before, but I put a "sticky note" with each of my boys' names on the wall beside my kitchen sink, praying, "God take care of my boys." I don't know why I did this, because they were all taken care of at that time.

"Lord, how do I help my Michael?"

I will continue to comfort you even though the doctors tell me that you don't know I'm there. I will tell you to wake up...then...I will keep telling you to fight and not give up. I am still trusting God to bring you back.

"Lord, have mercy!"

Friday, we have a meeting with the doctors again. There have been so many prayers from churches all over the world and from friends and family.

October 9

Bad News

The doctor said that you are paralyzed from the neck down. "Why? You were moving your arms before. What happened?!!" He also said your quality of life wouldn't be good. "But if your mind is there, I want you here. How could I give up when your mind is here?" Or is it?

"Please, God. I need you to tell me something, anything that will ease my pain. I thought you, God, were going to heal my son, so he at least could move his arms and still have a great mind as before and be able to see and talk. Oh, God, have mercy."

I read to you, "My soul, wait thou only upon God; for my expectation is from him. He only is my rock and my salvation: he is my defense, I shall not be moved. In God is my salvation and my glory: the rock of my strength and my refuge, is in God" (Psalm 62:5-7, KJV).

In the afternoon, I sang songs with you. "Jesus loves me," and, "This little light of mine," and "You are so beautiful." I prayed over you. You were resting. A mother's desperate plea:

"God, have mercy; to you, Lord, the glory. You will heal Michael, and to you, the glory will be."

October 10

When I came to see you this morning and as I do every time I see you, I cradled my arms over you, and I prayed close to your ear, so you will hear me and feel me close to you.

"My Little Star."

I prayed that all germs and diseases and curses to be taken out of your body in the name of Jesus.

I asked God to give me a sign that you can hear me. I asked you to move your head three times. I thought you did, ever so slightly that I could have even imagined it, but I didn't want to believe that. I praised God. I am so excited to see you later. I told you to fight and prove to these doctors that God healed you when they couldn't, and that I will not give up on you, or give up on God. God is healing you, Michael. We both believe that nothing is impossible with God. (Luke 1:37) ASB.

October 11

The neurology doctor was in this morning. He wants to do another brain scan. The physiotherapist and the nurse pressed and shook your chest, to loosen up your lungs and get you to cough. They have been doing this every day because you are unable to cough on your own.

Remember, Michael, these verses you texted me in the morning one day? "Although the fig tree shall not blossom, neither shall fruit be in the vines; the labour of the olive shall fail, and the fields shall yield no meat; the flock shall be cut off from the fold, and there shall be no herd in the stalls: Yet I will rejoice in the Lord, I will joy in the God of my salvation. The Lord God is my strength, and he will make my feet like hinds' feet, and he will make me to walk upon mine high places." (Habakkuk 3: 17-19, KJV). It so happened I had read the exact passage the night before you had sent them. That was so awesome!

I don't understand why there are ongoing tests to be taken. I don't get it. I take it as a sign that the doctors haven't given up yet, even though I was told your quality of life wouldn't be good, being paralyzed from the neck down.

I know that you wouldn't want to be in a state like this. You wouldn't want to live, having to be cared for in this manner. I am still trusting God.

Your eyes were checked and you followed eye commands. So, that is great! Your reflexes were checked, but there was no response. Your temperature seems to be stabilized, with no ice baths or cold air mattress.

I continue to pray and thank Jesus for healing you. I pray without ceasing. I tell you to fight as hard as you can, then rest, fight again, then rest. I know you are, and I am so proud of you, my precious son.

"God, have mercy."

I read to you, "God is our refuge and strength, a very present help in trouble" (Psalm 46:1, KJV).

October 12

Saturday

Today, you were very tired. You couldn't respond to the nurse's commands. You stayed awake for about an hour all day. But by your side, I was there, even when you slept. I prayed with you and read to you: "Hear my cry, O God, listen to my prayer. From the ends of the earth I call to You, I call as my heart grows faint; lead me to the Rock that is higher than I" (Psalm 61:1-2, KJV).

October 14

It's Thanksgiving and I am so thankful for my family, their strength and courage.

"My Sweetie, star of my heart."

This morning, I prayed with you, as I do many times a day. I will be faithful to God in prayer and thank him for healing you, be it his will. Could it possibly be his will, to take you from me? "Nothing is impossible with God" (Luke 1:37). To him be the glory!

I was talking to you about getting the tube removed from your mouth, so you could speak to me. But you are not well enough yet.

October 15

"Oh, God, have mercy. I know you are a just God."

This morning you were awake, just half an hour. The nurses were busy with you for most of the day. I didn't see too much of you today. Your MRI was taken between 2 and 4 p.m. When I saw you at 5 p.m. your eyes were open for two hours, which is so unusual for you, for so long. Usually, when your eyes are open, they want to close all the time. I read Psalms, chapter 91 to you. We can read it together, when you are well: "God is our stronghold." I sang to you how beautiful you are and how strong you are in the Lord, and that God had everything in control, even though times are excruciatingly hard to go through. I am so proud of you.

"I love you so much, Michael."

Remember we always prayed that God would use us to help others? I told all the nurses that God is healing you and their lives will be changed. No matter what people say, I will give God the glory.

October 16

What the doctor did was make an opening in your throat and put a breathing tube in it. So you can breathe that way. It looks terrible that you have to have that in your body. I don't like it at all. The doctor said you wouldn't be able to talk, because your vocal cords are not able to function yet, if ever, because of the respirator being in your mouth and throat for three weeks. And here I thought you could talk after it was removed.

"I am so confused, Lord. Why are things looking so bad? I pray, Lord, that Michael will be able to speak soon."

"Michael, my prayers are minute-by-minute, hour-to-hour. I have never trusted God more than I do right now."

"God have mercy!"

October 17

When I came to see you this morning, your face was beautiful and clear. Your stitches were taken out and looking good. You looked like yourself. Your eyes were open (you still can't see me) and that respirator is out of your mouth. It's in your throat on the outside. You looked like you were aware.

"Where are you my son? I want you to be here."

I read Psalms 31:1-3, "In thee, O LORD, do I put my trust; let me never be ashamed: deliver me in thy righteousness. Bow down thine ear to me; deliver me speedily; be though my strong rock, for an house of defense to save me. For thou art my rock and my fortress; therefore for thy name's sake lead me, and guide me (KJV).

I speak to you every day. "Putting on the full amour of God."

"I pray, Lord for courage and peace. Comfort Michael. I want to believe that Michael is strong in you, Lord, and not confused and in pain."

I am still trusting God, Michael.

There have been so many obstacles--like your temperature, kidneys, and heart—that you have overcome...But God has big plans for you, Michael. This is the test we shall pass. Remember that we spoke about the tests we go through and how God helps us through those trials? Anything from a personal problem to family and friends and other circumstances that are beyond us. How God is good. Remember we spoke about I Philippians 4:11, where Paul said he had become content in all circumstances? You loved that. You wanted to tattoo that, too. There were so many verses you wanted as tattoos.

"I love you."

5 PM

Your MRI results are in. I met with the neurologist and he said that you will not have use of your arms and legs and that you suffered a brain injury and only time will tell if you improve mentally. *"WHAT?"* When you were admitted, I heard you were joking around with the doctor that put your stitches in your forehead. I just can't accept this diagnosis. I don't want to accept it. I won't accept that you were mentally ill when you were admitted. You were not. I spoke to you on the phone and after your surgery, and you responded fine.

"Oh Lord, what do we do now?"

We all realized that you are getting worse and suffering so much. I will continue to pray.

"God, have mercy."

"I love you, Michael."

Throughout the night you developed a fever, but it broke this afternoon. Later in the day, the doctor said that the "trach" that they put in your throat was to be replaced for a bigger one, so you had to go back to surgery again. As if you were not going through enough already. Thank God, you came out of surgery.

Tonight, you look like you are very uncomfortable.

"Lord, help Michael and strengthen me."

"How can I leave you, Michael? Another night without you."

Your face muscles were twitching. I held you, wrapping my arms around you, your face on mine as I gently spoke in your ear,

"Everything will be OK. God is with you."

I have held you for hours this way, every day since you arrived at the hospital. I touch your face and stroke your forehead, as to close your eyes like you did as a child. You just loved that. I touched your moustache and little goatee, kissed your lips, your nose, each eye, and my nose on your eyelid, the way that you always liked, because you said it felt so cool. *"Your laugh so awesome, your heart so pure, your love so real. You are so precious."* You know that I have told you that you are my beautiful son, inside and out. I sang that song to you: "You are so beautiful to me," as I caress you closely. 'I pray, Michael, that you hear me and that you are not in any pain.

I will always talk to you. I just know in my heart that you know I am here with you.

I know you said so many times that you loved Aedan so much (you called him "that little guy with the sweet voice"), that he was so cute. Remember you said you couldn't wait to take him out and take him to church? Shane has a video of Aedan, for you to see and listen to. He played it for you at your bedside. He said, "Hi Michael. I miss you. I love you." And he throws you a kiss.

I know we have spoken so many times about the family. I know you have said that family is most important that everyone should get along with each other. That we should show love and tell each other, and "be there for each other," when there is a need. Now we are here for you, Michael.

October 18

I know how you respond to family trials…in a very loving way, not judging, but creating a loving atmosphere for everyone. I know we have prayed for our family and asked God to bring us closer together.

"I love you, my beautiful son. I will see you in the morning."

I am remembering you singing in church as we lifted our hands to Jesus. You loved to sing.

October 19

"Good morning, Sweetie. You looked well rested this morning. Yet still so sick."

You had many visitors today, a very emotional day for all of us. Seeing you so sick. Many, many tears of love.

Last night you had more problems with your heart. A very difficult night. The doctors had to immediately medicate you.

"Lord, have mercy."

I am so confused. I don't know what to think or do. I am almost numb with disbelief that this is happening to you, Michael.

"I know God is with you, but where are you, my son? Can you hear me anymore?"

I have still not stopped believing that God will get you well again and I don't want to believe otherwise. But truthfully, you are suffering and not getting any better.

These words I speak are words of desperation. I still encourage you to picture yourself well again, picturing Jesus, leaning on him and asking his Spirit to take over your thoughts and your body and heal your mind.

"God, have mercy."

October 20

This morning, Daniel sent for two of the pastors of our church in Abbotsford. They came to see you and pray with you and our family. You were not awake at the time. We prayed for God's will for your life, whether it would be healing you, or taking you home. I want you here so much but what if it wasn't God's will? How do I go on without you?

As the pastors left your room, I again prayed over you and sang to you, still encouraging you to fight. I wanted to see any glimmer of hope that you would come back to me. My mind tried to fathom the magnitude of what was happening through this journey for you Michael, and for our family.

It was extremely difficult this morning to see my "Little Star" so far away.

Your eyes are so beautiful but somewhere else, it seems.

I spoke to you with a heavy, heavy heart.

"Oh God, give me strength, I cannot bear this, to see my son detached. I want him back."

"I prayed with you, Sweetie, and my tears were unstoppable."

I sobbed and sobbed.

"Please God, have mercy. Bring Michael back to me."

"You are a blessing, courageous, strong and full of loving-kindness. I am so proud of you, Michael. I love you so."

The last two nights you have had no heart problems, although you are still on meds for that. Every day I hold you, hug you in my arms. I love you so. My heart aches for you.

Your body is still swelled up. You still can't see your veins and all of your muscles are gone, and you had a lot of them, because of your bodybuilding. Today, you took two breaths on your own. I thought it was a huge accomplishment, Sweetie. The nurse said she finally could document that little change.

"Thank you, Jesus."

Last night you had no change, but no added problems. But still your body is basically shutting down, little by little. You must be exhausted, my precious son. Later this day, your heart rate went way down, two different times. The first time the nurses got your heart rate back up quickly with medication. The second time, the nurses gave you the same medication, but it didn't work in getting your heart rate back up, so they had to double the meds. Your heart is failing rapidly, where meds are not enough. Your blood pressure then went way up, but they were able to stabilize everything. But doubling the medication is not good either.

"Oh, God, how do we help Michael?"

Things do not look good. Up until now, I have kept my tears to myself, leaving your bedside, but only for a moment, so as to not discourage you of any hope of recovery. But your symptoms are taking their toll on your body. As I cradled your face in my arms, I bawled my eyes out. You are so precious. You are looking around, but can't see anything.

"Oh, God."

My tears alone would have brought tears to yours, and I knew that you are saying to me not to worry: "Everything will be OK, Mom."

But, I am so scared of what is to come.

"Oh God, help me to cope with what is next. I have kept my faith and trusted you in what is best for Michael."

"My sweet Michael.""

Your family members talked, and decided that you were suffering too much, and so we decided to talk to the doctor and nurse about whether or not to take you off life support. We took into consideration the fact that your spinal cord injury has caused paralysis from your neck down, with no hope of recovery. You are unable to see or speak, and need to be on life support in order to breathe. We were sure that this was not the life that you want, or what we want for you. I am terrified, Michael, but God knows what is best. And as crazy as it sounds, I am still waiting for a miracle that all of a sudden you could see and talk again.

"The pain I feel for you is excruciating. I love you so much, like you always tell me 'tons and tons.'"

"Oh, Lord, help me through this. We need you now more than ever. It's hard to say 'Praise you, Jesus,' but you know more than we can possibly understand, and that you mean it for good. God have mercy. Give me comfort, Lord, knowing you are with Michael this very hour. Give me the peace in any decision that will be made and that it is the right one for my son, Michael, my precious boy."

October 21

This morning, you were awake when I came in to see you. I held you in my arms and sang songs softly into your ear. I just know you heard me and felt me there. The tremble in your lip stopped, as I sang. I spoke about Jesus and heaven. You had said to me a few months ago that you liked the sound of the word "home," when the Bible talked about heaven. "Remember? You had more faith and wisdom in your 23 years, than I had ever seen in anyone before."

The final meeting with the doctor and nurse

Walking into the "room of decision," I thought it would never come to this. I am terrified at losing you.

"Oh Lord, help me. This is so mind-altering and unreal to comprehend. Oh, God! Why? Why?"

My heart is screaming, *"This isn't right—Michael, you need to be here!"* But the doctor calmly explained the order in which you would leave us. As I left the room, my body felt so heavy, as if I was on a black cloud….it was all so surreal. Even though I knew in my heart and mind that there was no choice but to let you go to Jesus. You had suffered enough. But my heart cried out,

"Please, God, I need you!"

Deep, down inside, I knew it had been inevitable. And this brought God's peace and calm. He didn't want you to suffer any more.

"Oh God, my heart is physically aching beyond words."

"God has a plan. Sweetie, you have been an ambassador for Christ, and He says to you now, 'Michael, my good and faithful servant'."

As I spoke, my insides were trembling. I knew you would be in heaven soon. We are confident, I say, and willing rather to be absent from the body, and to be present with the Lord (II Corinthians 5:8, KJV).

This morning, you had another heart problem. We leave you in the hands of the Lord, as we have been doing all along. Right now, I feel strong and peaceful that you will be with Jesus. No more suffering.

"But Lord, help me through this. At times, I feel I am not comprehending what is happening. I am in shock."

"I love you, Michael, my beautiful son."

We called everyone to come and say good-bye to you the day before. I can't remember everyone that came, but your day was filled with family and friends. The gold chain that I had given to you years ago for your birthday, that you wore every day, that was taken off you when you came to the hospital. I had been wearing it every day since then, for safekeeping until you were better. I asked your best friend, Brad, if he would like your necklace, and he said that he would be honoured. So right there in the hospital room beside you, I took it off myself and placed it around his neck.

"I knew that's what you would have wanted, Michael."

I asked that our favorite nurse Ellen be present on the day of October 25, 2013. She was wonderful to you, Michael. She cared for you so lovingly.

The day of

This morning, your family gathered around your bed, and watched while the doctor and the nurse went about the process and steps that would be taken medically, to give you the most comfortable release to Jesus. All meds will be stopped and the breathing tube taken out. But before that you would be given anxiety meds, anesthetic and other drugs too, so you would not struggle to take your last breath on your own.

Psalm 23

"THE Lord is my shepherd; I shall not want.
He maketh me to lie down in green pastures; he leadeth me beside the still waters.

He restoreth my soul: he leadeth me in the paths of righteousness, for His name's sake.

Yea, though I walk through the valley of the shadow of death, I will fear no evil: for thou art with me; thy rod and thy staff, they comfort me.

Thou preparest a table before me in the presence of mine enemies: thou anointest my head with oil; my cup runneth over.

Surely goodness and mercy shall follow me all the days of my life: and I will dwell in the house of the LORD, forever" (KJV).

Aloud, I read Psalm 23, with tears that clouded my sight and with trembling hands that I could not control, as I read it to you. I then touched your little perfect toes. I held my head on your heart. I kissed your hands and slowly ran my fingers through your fingers. The fingers that had warmed me so many times before. Through my pool of tears, I kissed your little perfect ears, your nose, your lips, your forehead, and each eye. I kissed the little scar below your eye, where you hit yourself on a table when you were three years old. I cradled your head in my arms and sang, "You are so beautiful," and "Jesus loves the little children of the world."

It reminded me of sending you short videos of Aedan, and you texted back to me, "Thanks mom for not letting him forget me."

I quoted God's word, "Have I not commanded you? Be strong and courageous. Do not tremble or be dismayed, for the Lord your God is with you wherever you go" (Joshua 1:9).

As I stood at your bedside, trying to fathom what was happening and not even trying to fight back the tears anymore, God reassured me of your comfort. I cradled your head in my arms, telling you how proud I was of you that you had fought with everything you had, as I cried uncontrollably. I whispered in your ear,

"Guess what, Sweetie, we passed the test and kept our faith in God."

I told you that we were going to help you that you had suffered long enough, and it was time to be at peace and joy, in the presence of our Jesus.

My mind did not comprehend what was happening before me. As I watched the nurse undoing wires and disconnecting instruments, I felt like I was going to faint. Every sense of my being was ripping through my heart. This can't be happening!

But it is.

AFTERWORD

At Michael's "Celebration of Life," I was a confused mess, but I knew there was no question that I would go up front and speak about my son. Even at this point, I don't know exactly what I said. I must have still been in shock. I wasn't able to describe my son, Michael, without crying. Here is what I would like you to know about Michael:

About my son, Michael, and his love for God

Michael's legacy is a powerful testimony to those that knew him. He loved Jesus. He was a kind-hearted young man. When you met Michael, you would soon see his heart. He loved his family and said so, many times. He cried and laughed at the same time—his heart was so sensitive. When Shane asked him to be a groomsman at his wedding, Michael was touched and showed his emotion to me. He said, "I love my brothers so much," with a tear in his eye.

He was so personable. He always took time to talk to you. He loved children. He and I served in Guatemala in 2009, with a church group (Michael was 18 years old). It was there where the kids jumped all over him, when he played with them. He also worked to help maintain the orphanage property. He loved to work. He was dedicated and always "put all in" to whatever he was doing.

When he was nine, Michael would volunteer at the "Menno Home" with me, playing board games with the elderly. There were many times he would give to the homeless on the street. He was so thoughtful of everyone yet so very humble. He was very intelligent, and a young man of great character. His word was his handshake.

He loved everyone and would often say, "Let's do something nice for someone." Michael would bring his unsaved friends to church sometimes.

We were driving to Tim Horton's one day and there was a young man about 16, doing some landscaping. It was a hot day, and the young man was hot and sweaty, so we bought the boy an "iced cap." Michael gave him the cold drink, and the boy was so thankful. We both drove away laughing and teary-eyed at the same time. There are so many good things I could say about Michael, but there is not enough paper.

Michael and I were extremely close. We prayed for each other and our family that God would use us to bring them to know Jesus. Michael loved to hug others. He just loved so much that he had to express it through touch. He loved animals and was also a gifted artist. He could draw anything, and I am happy that I have two pieces of his artwork to treasure. His love for God was apparent, his life a testimony.

Michael was baptized when he was 14 years old. He had tattoos of the "fruit of the spirit" on his wrists and his favourite verse on his forearm, Romans 12:21, "Do not be overcome by evil but overcome evil with good." When he was about 14, he came home from school with a shaved head. He said there was a fundraiser at school, and he did it "for cancer." When I gave him a look of shock, he said, "That's OK. It's no big deal. It'll grow back, and I have lots of hats I can wear," he said, laughingly.

He surprised me one day with tickets to a Jeremy Camp concert. We went to see them and also went to a Newsboys concert together. Besides being inspired by their music, and finding a closer relationship with God, we had so much fun together!

At home, he would take my hands and dance with me and say, "I love you, Mom." At church, he would sing. Oh, how he loved to sing! He loved all kinds of music.

It was just several hours before the accident when we texted to each other, both of us leaving from work, to get home. We would text every day, sometimes Bible verses, to encourage each other. It was 11:30 p.m. We were going to "Skype" on the Monday, and he was going to tell me about his MRI results on his knee. We talked continually about him moving from BC, to be nearer to me and his brothers.

EPILOGUE: My strength, my God

"How, Lord, do I live each day without my son? I feel like I am going to lose my mind completely. My reality is a daily nightmare. This can't be where I will stay all of my life? I am an emotional wreck and want out of this despair." I used to say,

"Lord, You are enough,"

... but now I question:

"Are you enough? I can't see a way out."

When I arrived home, I was overcome with grief. I wailed. I had never known what that was. It was a cry so deep I had never known before.

I was desperate to get help. I asked God,

"How do I live without my son? How do I smile again?"

The only place I knew was to run to God, desperately seeking strength. This verse came to me: "Come near to God and he will come near to you" (James 4:8, BBE).

Going through this nightmare, I found a deeper relationship with God. To get through this, I committed myself, forcing myself, to continually trust God. I was questioning God…. *"Why Lord?"* He told me that I wouldn't understand, and I didn't. I still don't. But he did tell me that he was in control of my life and he would help me through it.

I would cry myself to sleep at night, and awaken many times during the night, crying about my son. In the morning when I awoke, the devastation overwhelmed me. I asked God to help me.

I read God's word every day, through endless tears that sometimes soaked the pages I read. As time went on, I missed Michael even more. I journalled every day through the first year after Michael's release to Jesus. Sometimes the only entry for a day was, *"Help me, Jesus."*

I went to a counselor weekly. My doctor was also a support. I attended "Grief Share"--Christian support group meetings--and although it was extremely difficult to share my feelings, it was good to be with other parents who had lost children. However, at the group, it all seemed too real. At home by myself, it was hard to comprehend that this was actually true, that Michael really was gone. His photo seemed to be everywhere—on the walls, on my coffee table—but he's not there! It was mind blowing, especially the first day back to my home.

Although nothing takes the pain away, I still have to go through it each day, all day. There is a darkness in my heart that lingers about in whatever I do, whether it is in brushing my teeth, or celebrating birthdays. I read Bible verses on God's promises, and searched scriptures on heaven. I needed reassurance on where Michael was.

I didn't want to do anything or go anywhere for months. Sometimes I couldn't even get out of bed. I still have some of those days.

I forced myself to go to church, and as time went on, it was easier to attend, but only some days. Just by being with other people who believed in God the way I do, I gained strength. The music was especially difficult, but encouraging, knowing that Michael loved the music and loved to sing. He would have wanted to be there. "Mount up on wings like eagles…" was a song that Michael and I loved to sing in church.

Today, just short of two years later, I have gained a new strength, a new peace through God's grace. I know that God is always with me. I just know, because without his grace, I wouldn't have made it through. I'm still here, where I once thought I would go crazy. God has helped me live through this pain. He is my Rock. He loves me and has always had a plan for my life. He knows what's best for me, even though I don't understand all of it. If I had my choice, Michael would still be here…and we'd still be dancing.

"Oh God, how I need you!"

These verses give me strength, "Trust in the Lord with all your heart, do not lean on your own understanding. In all your ways acknowledge Him and He will make your paths straight" (Proverbs 3:5-6). "I can do all things through Christ, who strengthens me" (Philippians 4:13, NASB).

Today, I am stronger in my faith. Had I not gone through this, I wouldn't have experienced a deeper relationship with God. He is faithful. He is my God. He is my guide, my comfort, my peace and my joy. And I will see my son, Michael, again.

"Oh, God, how I need you!"

My strength truly comes from the Lord. He has brought me through so many losses in my life—my brother, my sister, my mom, my grandparents, and dear friends. Even though I had all these important losses in my life, they don't compare to the loss of my son. Those losses I have experienced are years past, but God's grace got me through. I have grown much more in my faith since then. God prepared my heart for what was to come. His grace sustains me.

Michael's death sent me straight to God's Word. I couldn't stop reading. I would become completely focused on God, rather than what was happening in my life.

"Thank you God, for the 23 wonderful years I had with Michael."

I will treasure all those wonderful memories of us....I miss you, Michael, with every breath that I take... I will meet you in heaven my precious son.

Love, M☺M

AFTERNOTES

The loss of my nephew was one of the hardest things I've had to deal with in my life for several reasons....My sister's pain was so horrible. I saw her die inside. I cried so often for her, I thought she too would leave us, over a broken heart. I'm so glad she trusts in God. Michael was the lifesaver for my son, Jeremy, when he went through a difficult time in his teenage years. Michael gave him strength when no one else could. My son, Joel, still has his picture on his dresser. He does not say much. But his silent tears are always there when we talk of Michael. He was truly a son moms pray for and dream about! I believe in my heart that God took him to be his angel. There is no other reason. He was just so special and a God's true son.... Garry

+++++++++++++

I miss my grandson, Michael. He was a joy to be around. I have no doubt where Michael is, and that is with the Lord. My faith has not been shaken. In this fallen world, Michael is in a much better place.... Grandpa

+++++++++++++

I see the evidence of the love that people showed to Michael. They spoke highly of him. He definitely made a difference in people's lives. To watch Michael want to live for the Lord was impressive to me. He was a very kind young man, being concerned for his mom, when he himself was being treated after the accident happened. He made sure his mom would drive safely. That's Michael....concern for others first.... Diane

+++++++++++++

After Michael's death, I watched Dianne "lean into" her faith, day after day. It supported her and changed our perspective on life experiences. Day-to-day we think we have important problems, but they are nothing compared to Dianne's loss. What a journey for her! I tried to be a good listener for her. That was about all I could do as her friend, besides be "on call" for her..... Betty

+++++++++++++

My brother's passing has made me look at how I express myself to people, as well as being more open to showing and voicing my love and appreciation for the people closest to me.

This was something Michael was very good at, and something I didn't appreciate as much as I should have. Two weeks before his accident, I was at least able to tell him how proud I was of him, and to see how much he appreciated me saying that was something special, and I only wish I had more opportunities to let him know how I loved and appreciated him for just being who he was …..Shane

++++++++++++

*In loving memory of Michael
Paul Randy Vanderploeg*